EARLY AMERICAN HISTORY

America's Westward Expansion

By Bert Wilberforce

Published in 2024 by Cavendish Square Publishing, LLC
2544 Clinton Street Buffalo, NY 14224

Website: cavendishsq.com

Library of Congress Cataloging-in-Publication Data

Names: Wilberforce, Bert, author. | Roza, Greg. Westward expansion.
Title: America's westward expansion / Bert Wilberforce.
Description: Buffalo, New York : Cavendish Square Publishing, [2024] |
Series: The inside guide: Early American history | Includes index.
Identifiers: LCCN 2022052959 (print) | LCCN 2022052960 (ebook) | ISBN 9781502667847 (library binding) | ISBN 9781502667830 (paperback) | ISBN 9781502667854 (ebook)
Subjects: LCSH: United States–Territorial expansion–Juvenile literature. | West (U.S.)–History–Juvenile literature. | West (U.S.)–Discovery and exploration–Juvenile literature. | Frontier and pioneer life–West (U.S.)–Juvenile literature.
Classification: LCC F591 .W697 2024 (print) | LCC F591 (ebook) | DDC 978/.02–dc23/eng/20221109
LC record available at https://lccn.loc.gov/2022052959
LC ebook record available at https://lccn.loc.gov/2022052960

Editor: Therese Shea
Designer: Deanna Paternostro

The photographs in this book are used by permission and through the courtesy of: Cover, pp. 7 (left and right), 10, 14 (inset), 15, 16 Everett Collection/Shutterstock.com; pp. 4, 21 Courtesy of the Library of Congress; p. 6 (main) Weft/Wikimedia Commons; p. 6 (inset) Themadchopper/Wikimedia Commons; pp. 8-9 Yeeno/Wikimedia Commons; p. 12 Leonard Zhukovsky/Shutterstock.com; pp. 13, 14 (main) Courtesy of the National Park Service, U.S. Department of the Interior; p. 18 Hpav7/Wikimedia Commons; p. 19 Taterian/Wikimedia Commons; p. 20 Noahedits/Wikimedia Commons; p. 22 North Wind Picture Archives/Alamy Stock Photo; p. 23 Schwabenblitz/Shutterstock.com; pp. 24 (main and inset) Courtesy of the National Archives; p. 25 Rjensen/Wikimedia Commons; p. 26 Fma12/Wikimedia Commons; p. 27 Victorian Traditions/Shutterstock.com; p. 29 (left) Entheta/Wikimedia Commons; p. 29 (right) Artanisen/Wikimedia Commons.

CPSIA compliance information: Batch #CSCSQ24: For further information contact Cavendish Square Publishing LLC at 1-877-980-4450.

Printed in the United States of America

CONTENTS

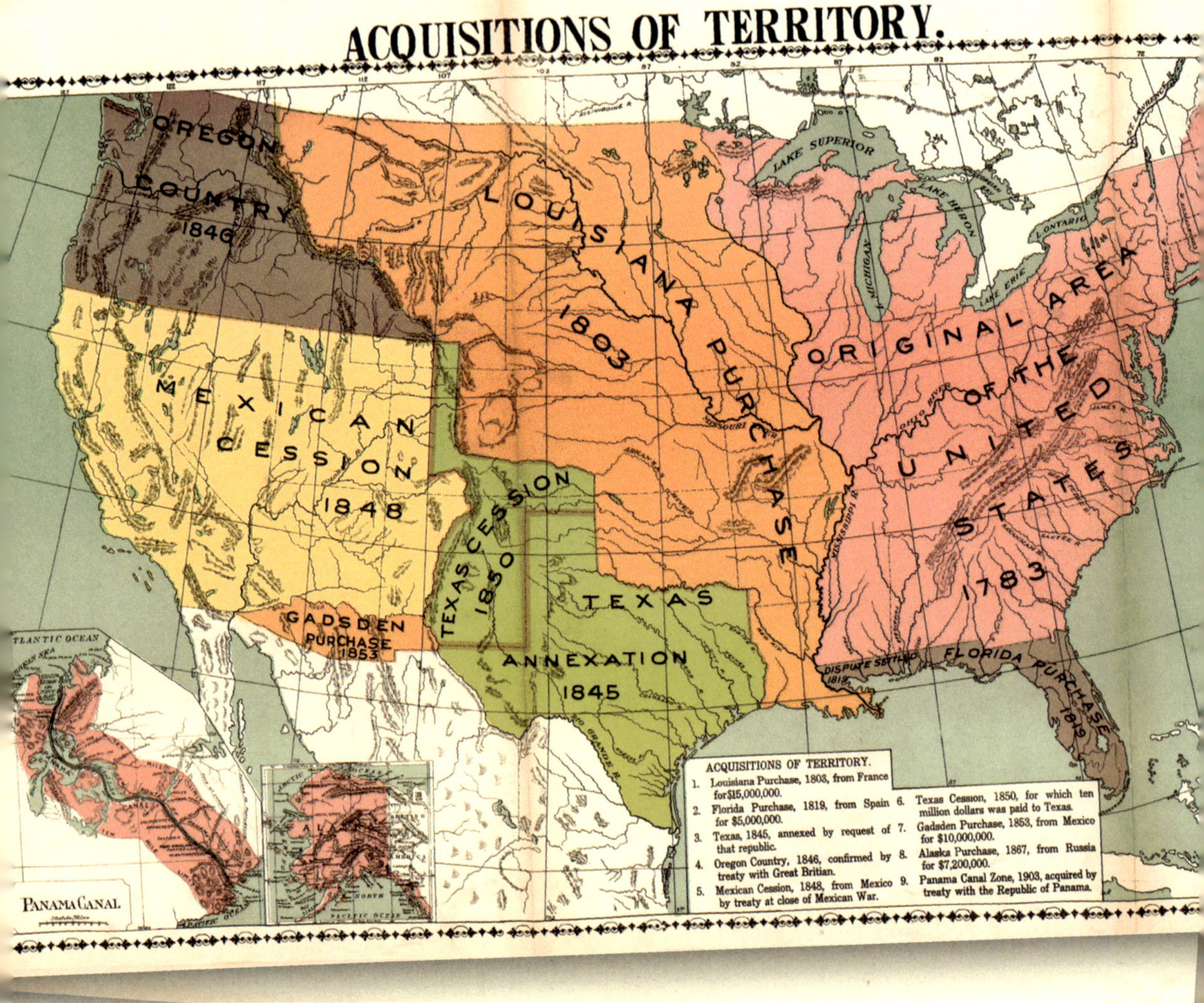

ACQUISITIONS OF TERRITORY.

ACQUISITIONS OF TERRITORY.

1. Louisiana Purchase, 1803, from France for$15,000,000.
2. Florida Purchase, 1819, from Spain for $5,000,000.
3. Texas, 1845, annexed by request of that republic.
4. Oregon Country, 1846, confirmed by treaty with Great Britian.
5. Mexican Cession, 1848, from Mexico by treaty at close of Mexican War.
6. Texas Cession, 1850, for which ten million dollars was paid to Texas.
7. Gadsden Purchase, 1853, from Mexico for $10,000,000.
8. Alaska Purchase, 1867, from Russia for $7,200,000.
9. Panama Canal Zone, 1903, acquired by treaty with the Republic of Panama.

The expansion of the United States was rapid, as this 1919 map shows.

EXPANDING BOUNDARIES

On September 3, 1783, the United States and Great Britain signed the Treaty of Paris. This agreement ended the American Revolution. In it, Great Britain accepted the United States as an independent nation. The treaty also made the Mississippi River the western boundary of the new country, but it was not long before Americans looked beyond this border, toward the west.

The age of westward expansion was beginning. During this time, the U.S. government obtained more and more land in western North America. American citizens, including **immigrants**, traveled west and settled there until the United States stretched from coast to coast.

Fast Fact

Land **ordinances** in the late 18th century established laws for measuring, distributing, and settling land. The Northwest Ordinance of 1787 led to the formation of five states from the **Northwest Territory**—Michigan, Indiana, Wisconsin, Ohio, and Illinois—as well as part of Minnesota.

A Large Purchase

By 1800, U.S. settlers—mostly merchants, trappers, loggers, and farmers—relied heavily on the Mississippi River and the port of New Orleans for transportation and **commerce**. Many Americans had even settled in areas west

Treaty
Between the United States of America and the French Republic

This is the treaty in which France gave control of the Louisiana Territory to the United States.

of the Mississippi, which Spain had recently sold to France. President Thomas Jefferson quickly recognized how important the river, port, and western lands were to the future of the U.S. economy.

In 1801, Jefferson sent a representative to France to purchase New Orleans and receive permission to use the Mississippi River. At first, France refused. However, two years later, French officials surprised Jefferson by offering to sell the entire Louisiana Territory to the United States for $15 million. Through the

Fast Fact

The United States bought the Louisiana Territory for less than 3 cents an acre (0.4 hectare).

This painting shows the U.S. flag being raised in New Orleans, replacing the French flag.

THE CORPS OF DISCOVERY

In 1803, President Jefferson organized an expedition to explore the Louisiana Territory and beyond, even before the land was purchased from France. Army officers Meriwether Lewis and William Clark led a small company called the Corps of Discovery over thousands of miles of uncharted land. The explorers, including a Shoshone woman named Sacagawea, mapped a route to the Pacific Ocean and met many groups of Native Americans along the way. They recorded information about the land and wildlife they encountered as well. The expedition helped raise interest among American citizens in settling land in the West.

Fast Fact

The Lewis and Clark expedition traveled over 8,000 miles (12,875 kilometers) in all.

Meriwether Lewis (*above left*), William Clark (*above right*), and other members of the Corps of Discovery kept detailed journals of their travels.

Louisiana Purchase, the size of the United States doubled.

Manifest Destiny

Some Americans believed that westward expansion—the movement and settlement of U.S. citizens in western lands—was necessary for the United States. The West had abundant natural resources, and more resources meant more wealth for the growing nation and its people. As more people moved west, the idea of Manifest Destiny became popular. Manifest Destiny was the belief that the United States had a mission to extend its western border to the Pacific Ocean.

Many credit journalist John L. O'Sullivan for coining the term in 1845 as he wrote in support of the **annexation** of Texas and California. O'Sullivan said other countries sought to limit the greatness of the United States by "checking the fulfillment of our manifest destiny to overspread the continent allotted by **Providence** for the free development of our yearly multiplying millions."

"Manifest Destiny" became a rallying cry for some, used by those who supported political and military missions to expand the borders of the United States.

Fast Fact

"Manifest" means "clear to understand." The word "destiny" refers to events that will happen in the future without doubt.

This 1872 painting, *American Progress*, shows a spirit representing the United States leading settlers westward. While Native Americans are depicted in the bottom left corner, the reality is they were pushed off their lands as white Americans moved west.

The building of the Erie Canal made travel easier between the Great Lakes and the Atlantic Ocean. It inspired other states to build their own canals.

CANALS AND TRAILS

Though many Americans wanted to settle in the West in the early 1800s, the journey was slow, hard, and sometimes dangerous, or unsafe. New routes and modes of transportation were necessary to cut down the time and danger as well as the cost of travel and shipping. Canals were one answer to this need.

The Erie Canal

The Erie Canal, built in New York State between 1817 and 1825, connected the Hudson River to Lake Erie. It was the first east–west water route in the nation. The canal made it quicker, cheaper, and easier to travel to and from the frontier west of the Appalachian Mountains.

The completion of the Erie Canal marked the first great western **migration** of American settlers. Communities along the canal—such as Albany, Syracuse, and Rochester—quickly grew into important cities. Buffalo became a vital destination for midwestern farmers who needed to ship wheat to the East and get supplies from New York City. The Erie Canal helped western farms and eastern cities thrive.

Fast Fact

The Erie Canal was 363 miles (584 km) long. The canal was later made wider and deeper for larger boats.

The original Erie Canal used 83 locks, or gated sections, to raise and lower ships between stretches of water of different levels.

The Oregon Territory and Trail

The Oregon Territory was an area of land in the Pacific Northwest that included the modern states of Oregon, Washington, and Idaho, as well as parts of Montana and Wyoming. Both the United States and Great Britain claimed this area at one time.

By 1846, many pioneers had already settled in what would become the Oregon Territory. Most reached the area by means of an overland route that came to be called the Oregon Trail. It started in Missouri and ended more than 2,000 miles (3,219 km) away in Oregon's Willamette Valley.

President James K. Polk pushed to make this area part of the United States. In 1846, Great Britain and the United States signed the Oregon Treaty, making the 49th **parallel** the official northern border of the United States in the West and ending joint occupation of the area.

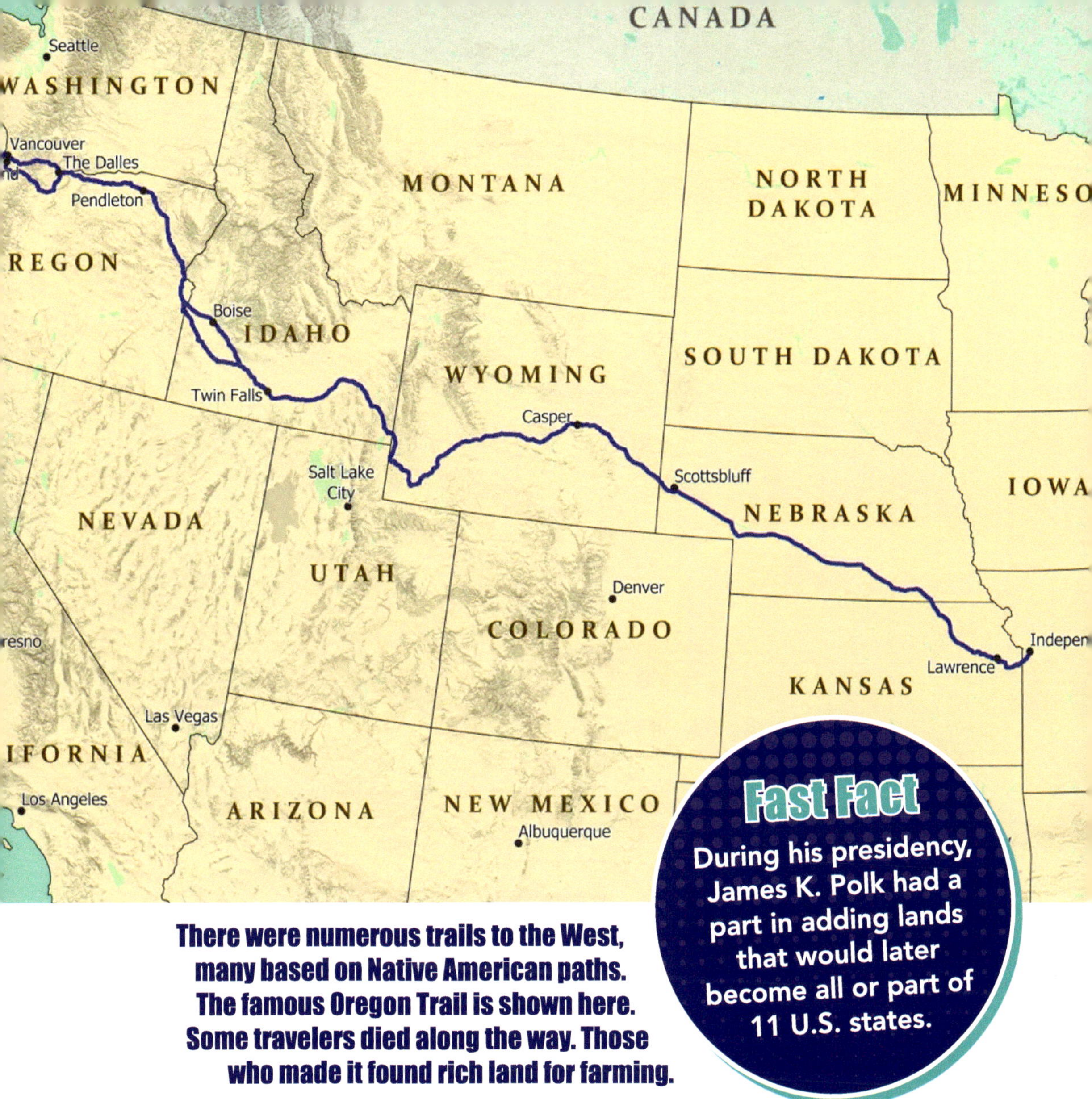

There were numerous trails to the West, many based on Native American paths. The famous Oregon Trail is shown here. Some travelers died along the way. Those who made it found rich land for farming.

Fast Fact

During his presidency, James K. Polk had a part in adding lands that would later become all or part of 11 U.S. states.

The Mormon Trail

The Church of Jesus Christ of Latter-day Saints began in 1830 in Fayette, New York. Although membership grew quickly, some did not like the new religion. The Church's members, sometimes called Mormons, headed west in search of a friendlier place to live. From 1839 to 1846, they lived in the city of Nauvoo in Illinois. However, hostilities, or unkind treatment, against them soon forced them to go farther west.

Latter-day Saint leaders, including Brigham Young, selected the Great Salt Lake region of today's Utah as their destination. They traveled a path about 1,300 miles (2,092 km) long that became known as the Mormon Trail. After a difficult journey, they founded Salt Lake City on July 24, 1847.

Fast Fact

By 1852, about 20,000 members of the Church of Jesus Christ of Latter-day Saints had arrived at Salt Lake Valley.

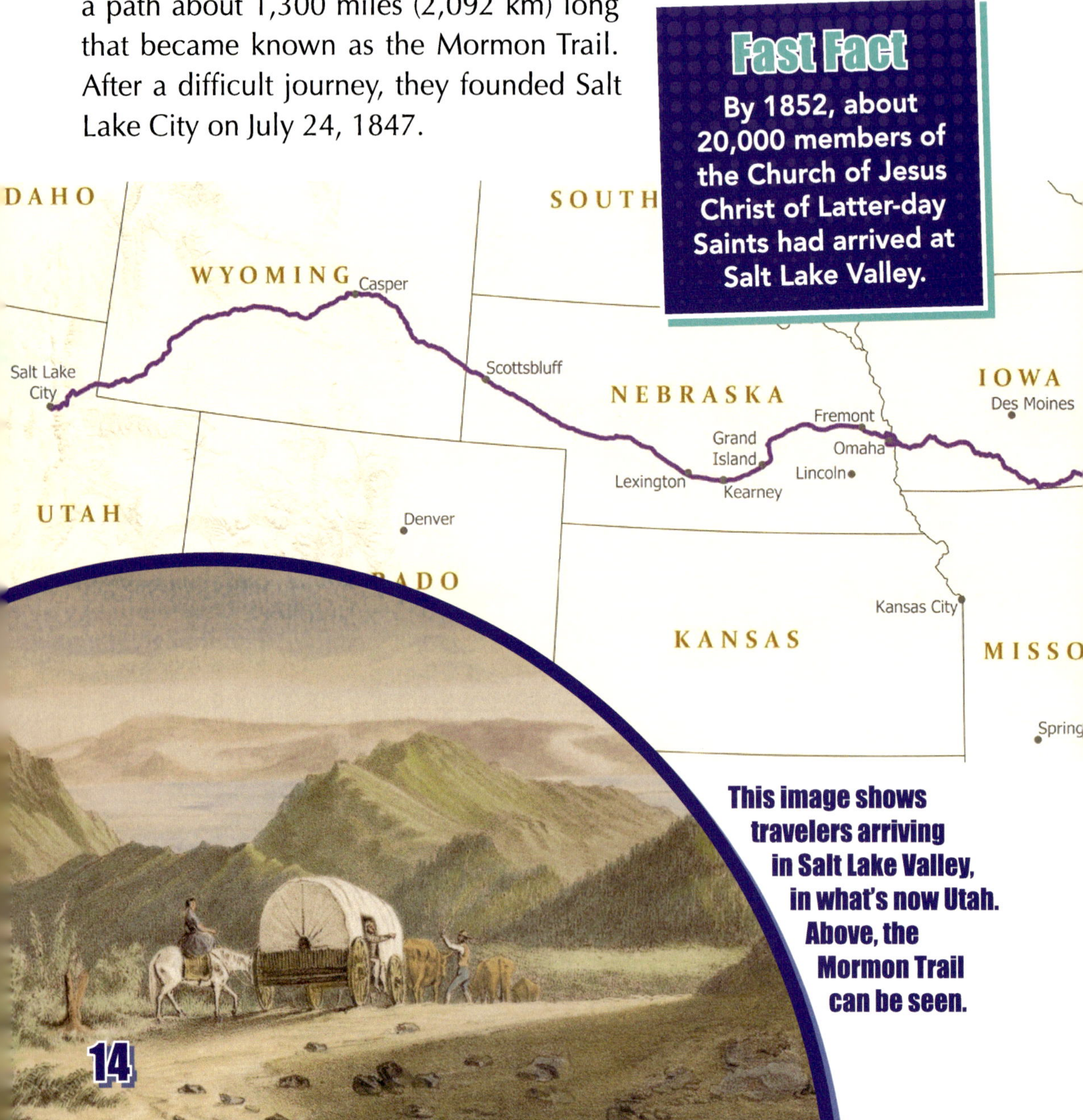

This image shows travelers arriving in Salt Lake Valley, in what's now Utah. Above, the Mormon Trail can be seen.

TENSIONS WITH NATIVE AMERICANS

Members of the Church of Latter-day Saints became the first non–Native Americans to settle in Salt Lake Valley, but the Ute people were already there. A war between the two groups eventually broke out as they competed for land and natural resources. The Ute people were pushed off their historic lands. Similar events would happen to Native Americans living across North America. Many were forced onto **reservations**, sometimes hundreds of miles from where they had lived, and made to give up important parts of their **cultures**, including their languages. Sometimes those who refused to obey were killed.

Conflict occurred between settlers too. In an incident called the Mountain Meadows Massacre in 1857, disguised Latter-day Saints and some Paiute allies attacked another group of pioneers passing through Utah.

The Battle of the Alamo in 1836 was one of the most famous battles in the Texas Revolution. Nearly all the Texans defending the former mission in San Antonio were killed.

ADDING TEXAS AND CALIFORNIA

The Spanish were early European explorers of the areas that are today's Texas and California. These, along with much of the Southwest and Mexico, became part of a Spanish colony called New Spain in 1535.

In 1821, Mexico, which then included Texas, won its independence from Spain. Both Spain and Mexico allowed Anglo-Americans, or Americans of English background, to settle in Texas around this time. Thousands arrived—about 25,000 by 1830. However, these settlers would soon clash with the Mexican government.

From Independence to Statehood

Texas colonists fought the Mexican army in what is now called the Texas Revolution between October 1835 and April 1836. The colonists declared Texas an independent nation. However, Texas struggled to defend itself against Mexico. Its economy also struggled.

Fast Fact

Though the Texans were defeated at the Alamo during the Texas Revolution, "Remember the Alamo" became a famous rallying cry.

Some members of Texas's government asked the U.S. government to annex Texas. In 1845, the U.S. Congress agreed to make Texas a state.

Rumors of an upcoming war between Mexico and the United States began soon after.

War with Mexico

The U.S. annexation of Texas angered the Mexican government, which had never recognized Texas's independence. In addition, the United States and Mexico both claimed the territory between the Rio Grande and the Nueces River. U.S. president James K. Polk tried to purchase the land and other territory secretly from Mexico at first but was rejected.

The Treaty of Guadalupe Hidalgo gave the United States territory that includes all or part of today's states of New Mexico, Utah, Nevada, Arizona, California, Texas, Colorado, Wyoming, Kansas, and Oklahoma. In return, the United States gave Mexico $15 million.

Fast Fact

In 1854, the United States paid Mexico $10 million for about 30,000 square miles (77,700 sq km) of land in northern Mexico. This is now southern Arizona and southern New Mexico. The Gadsden Purchase, as it is called, is shown on this map.

In April 1846, Mexican troops crossed the Rio Grande to attack American forces, starting the Mexican-American War. Battles during the war took place in Texas, California, and Mexico. In September 1847, U.S. forces reached Mexico City. Soon after, Mexico surrendered. In 1848, U.S. and Mexican officials signed the Treaty of Guadalupe Hidalgo, which officially ended the war.

The California Gold Rush

Just days before the Treaty of Guadalupe Hidalgo was signed, transferring California from Mexico to the United States, gold was discovered in California. News about the gold spread quickly across the nation and around the world. By 1849, people had flocked to the site and other areas in hopes of becoming wealthy. They were called forty-niners. California was made a state just a year later, in 1850.

By 1853, about 250,000 people had arrived in California to mine gold.

Fast Fact

California Native Americans numbered about 150,000 before the gold rush. About 20 years later, just about 30,000 remained. Disease and mistreatment had killed thousands in a short period of time.

Though most people did not find their fortune in the goldfields, many decided to settle in California, and the population rose quickly. One of the largest groups of immigrants came from China. Although they were often treated with **prejudice**, Chinese Americans made important contributions to the growing cities of California.

So many Native Americans died in California following the gold rush—including thousands murdered or enslaved—that some people call the actions of that time the California genocide.

BOOMTOWNS

As the California gold rush died down, miners searched other western areas for their fortunes. In 1859, silver ore was found on Mount Davidson in Utah Territory (in the area that is now Nevada). Henry Comstock claimed to own the land, so the deposit became known as the Comstock **Lode**. As people came to strike it rich, nearby "boomtowns," such as Virginia City, grew quickly. For close to 20 years, miners continued to find silver. In time, however, just as with the gold in California, the Comstock Lode ran out. Many of the boomtowns of the past dwindled as miners left. However, many people settled in the area permanently.

This drawing shows how miners worked underground. Wooden structures were in place to keep the mines from collapsing. Mills to crush the ore are also shown.

White Americans began to settle on the Great Plains, shown on the map, in larger numbers after 1862.

A SPREADING POPULATION

By the mid-1800s, the United States had spread to the West Coast, but some parts of the country weren't populated by many white settlers yet. Certain events, however, would encourage more settlement. One was a U.S. law signed in 1862. It became one of the most effective tools to spur migration.

The Homestead Act

In 1862, President Abraham Lincoln signed the Homestead Act into law. It allowed citizens to settle and farm on the Great Plains for "free." Each settler was given 160 acres (65 ha) of federally owned land. The settler had to live on and farm the land for five years before they became the legal owner. Or, after living on the land for six months, they could buy it for $1.25 an acre.

HOMESTEAD.

Land Office at Brownville

January 20

CERTIFICATE, No. 1

It is hereby certified, That pursuant to the provisions of the act of Congre

20, 1862, entitled "An act to secure homesteads to actual settlers on the public domain,"

Daniel Freeman

in Township four

containing 160

Now, therefore, be it known, That on presentation of this Cert

OF THE GENERAL LAND OFFICE, the said Dani

shall be entitled to a Patent for the Tract of Land above

This certificate is a record of homesteader Daniel Freeman's successful claim, five years after he first settled his land.

However, homestead life on the Great Plains was difficult. Much of the land was dry, dusty, and not suited to farming. And many homesteaders did not know much about farming. In some areas, dust storms made homestead life unbearable. Still, the Homestead Act of 1862 was considered a success. About 270 million acres (109 million ha) were settled.

Cattle Towns

The cattle industry was another reason for settlement. In the 1850s, cattle worth $10 a

Fast Fact

About 4 million people tried to settle land through the Homestead Act. However, only about 1.6 million deeds were successfully claimed.

A child feeds chickens on a Montana homestead around 1910.

Cattle drives like this were possible because of the open range north of Texas. Gradually, homesteaders took over (and fenced in) this land.

head in Texas could sell for 20 times more on the West Coast. Ranch owners raised herds of tens of thousands of cattle on large ranches. Several times a year, they hired cowboys to lead cattle drives north along trails to markets or, later, railroad stations hundreds of miles away. Many of the "cattle towns" (or cow towns) where north–south cattle trails and east–west railroads met grew into important cities. Abilene and Wichita in Kansas were settled this way.

Fast Fact

Spanish settlers were raising cattle as early as 1500 in North America. The Spanish also brought horses to the Americas.

Between 1866 and 1890, more than 5 million head of cattle were driven on cattle trails. However, toward the end of that time, more railroads and refrigerated railcars made cattle drives unnecessary.

A Transcontinental Train Route

Throughout the first half of the 1800s, the construction of railroads in the Northeast was steady and productive. The West, however, was untouched by railroads.

On May 10, 1869, the first **transcontinental** railroad in the United States was completed. The line connected the East and West, making travel

The transcontinental railroad was built across mountains and deserts, areas that were difficult for settlers to travel through.

Fast Fact

The transcontinental railroad reduced the time it took to cross the United States from months to less than a week.

easier, safer, and quicker. It sped up the rate at which the West was populated by white settlers, bringing more and more people every year. Soon, people could reach just about any location in the United States on newly built railroads. Towns and businesses were established along the lines. A frontier land unsettled by white Americans largely ceased to exist in the United States, and the era of westward expansion drew to an end.

THE OKLAHOMA LAND RUSH

The last major event of westward expansion in the United States is sometimes called the Oklahoma land rush. In 1834, the Indian Territory (now Oklahoma) had been set aside for Native American groups that had been forcibly relocated from their eastern lands, especially the Choctaw, Creek (Muscogee), Seminole, Cherokee, and Chickasaw peoples. However, pressure built to allow white settlers to have the Indian Territory too. In 1889, the U.S. government opened approximately 2 million acres (809,371 ha). Settlers raced to claim land, some rushing in early and illegally. These lands became the Oklahoma Territory, and in 1907, the Indian and Oklahoma Territories became the state of Oklahoma.

This photograph was taken just seconds after a gunshot signaled the beginning of the Oklahoma land rush in April 1889. About 50,000 people raced to claim land.

A TIMELINE OF WESTWARD EXPANSION

1783 The United States and Great Britain sign the Treaty of Paris.

1787 The Northwest Ordinance provides a way for new states to be formed from the Northwest Territory.

1803 The United States purchases the Louisiana Territory from France. The Lewis and Clark Expedition explores a route through it to the Pacific.

1820 Moses Austin gets permission to settle Anglo-American families in Texas.

1825 The Erie Canal opens.

1836 Texas declares itself independent from Mexico.

1845 John L. O'Sullivan uses the term "manifest destiny." Texas becomes the 28th U.S. state.

1846 Great Britain and the United States sign the Oregon Treaty.

1847 The Mexican-American War ends. The first members of the Church of Latter-day Saints arrive in the Utah Territory.

1848 Gold is found in California. U.S. and Mexican representatives sign the Treaty of Guadalupe Hidalgo.

1854 The United States acquires more territory through the Gadsden Purchase.

1859 Miners find the Comstock Lode in the Utah Territory.

1862 The Homestead Act is passed.

1866 The era of cattle drives from Texas begins.

1869 The first U.S. transcontinental railroad is completed.

1889 The Oklahoma land rush takes place.

THINK ABOUT IT!

1. Why do you think Spain and Mexico welcomed Anglo-Americans to Texas at first?
2. Why might Americans in the East have been drawn to a new life in the West, despite the dangers and hardships of the journey?
3. What is your opinion of the Manifest Destiny idea, and why?
4. How is western expansion linked to Native American history?

GLOSSARY

annexation: The addition of land to a country or region.

commerce: The large-scale buying and selling of goods and services.

culture: The beliefs and ways of life of a group of people.

genocide: The planned killing of people who belong to a certain race, nationality, or cultural group.

immigrant: Someone who moves into a new country from another country.

lode: A deposit of ore.

migration: The act of moving from one area to another.

Northwest Territory: Lands in the early history of the United States below the Great Lakes, west of Pennsylvania, northwest of the Ohio River, and east of the Mississippi River.

ordinance: A law or rule.

parallel: An imaginary line around Earth that is always the same distance away from the equator.

prejudice: An unfair feeling of dislike for someone or a group because of their race, sex, religion, or other feature.

Providence: Supposed guidance from God.

reservation: Land set aside by the U.S. government for Native Americans to live on.

transcontinental: Extending across a continent.

FIND OUT MORE

Books

Henzel, Cynthia Kennedy. *Manifest Destiny and the Journey West*. New York, NY: AV2 by Weigl, 2020.

Sebree, Chet'la, and Rebecca Stefoff. *Historical Sources on Westward Expansion*. New York, NY: Cavendish Square Publishing, 2020.

Yomtov, Nel. *The Louisiana Purchase: Asking Tough Questions*. North Mankato, MN: Capstone Press, 2021.

Websites

Westward Expansion
education.nationalgeographic.org/resource/resource-library-westward-expansion
Find valuable maps on this *National Geographic* site that will help you see the growth of the nation.

Westward Expansion and the Old West
www.ducksters.com/history/westward_expansion/
Read about some of the famous figures of the western frontier, including Daniel Boone, Sam Houston, and Annie Oakley.

Westward Expansion: Encounters at a Cultural Crossroads
www.loc.gov/classroom-materials/westward-expansion-encounters-at-a-cultural-crossroads/
The Library of Congress offers many primary sources, including photographs, related to western settlement.

Publisher's note to educators and parents: Our editors have carefully reviewed these websites to ensure that they are suitable for students. Many websites change frequently, however, and we cannot guarantee that a site's future contents will continue to meet our high standards of quality and educational value. Be advised that students should be closely supervised whenever they access the internet.

INDEX

EARLY AMERICAN HISTORY

TITLES IN THE SERIES

The American Revolution

America's Westward Expansion

Native Americans in Early America

Slavery in America

The Story of Immigration and Migration

The 13 Colonies